SURVIVAL SKILLS FOR KIDS

Published by
GRAPEVINE BOOKS

www.grapevinebooks.com
email: contact@grapevinebooks.com

Ordering Information:
Quantity sales: Special discounts are available on quantity purchases by corporations, associations, and others. For details, reach out to the publisher.

First published by Grapevine Books 2025

What is SURVIVAL?

Welcome, Junior Explorer!

Imagine you're walking through a quiet forest with your backpack on, the wind whispering in the trees, birds calling in the distance, and suddenly, you realize... you can't find your way back.

Would you panic?
Would you freeze?
Or would you stop, take a breath, and use what you know?

That last option; that calm, smart response is what survival is all about.

Survival doesn't mean fighting bears or living off bugs. It means using your mind, your eyes, your skills, and your calm heart to stay safe, find help, and solve problems when things don't go as planned.
This book is your adventure guide.
Your brain is your most important survival tool.

Let's sharpen it together.

What You'll Learn

So, what exactly will you learn in this book?

Well, you'll learn how to think like a survivor, how to respond instead of panic, and how to stay safe and smart in almost any outdoor situation.

You'll discover how to build a shelter out of branches and leaves, how to find water if your bottle runs dry, how to use a compass to point your way home, and what to do if you ever get lost or stuck. You'll learn how to read the sky, spot useful plants (and dangerous ones), tie knots that can hold up a tent, and even send signals if you need help.

But this isn't just a "how-to" manual. It's an invitation to become something bigger—someone who's prepared, thoughtful, calm, and brave. Every single chapter gives you not just facts, but hands-on challenges, mini missions, real-life stories, and brainpower games to put your survival smarts to the test.

By the end of this journey, you'll know how to:

Build your own survival kit
Handle small emergencies
Think clearly when things go wrong
Be a confident explorer

And the best part?
You'll realize that the greatest survival skill of all... is already inside you.

What isn't SURVIVAL

When some people hear the word survival, they imagine something wild and dramatic—like swinging from vines, wrestling bears, or eating bugs to stay alive. But here's the truth: that's not what survival is really about.

Real survival is not a dare, a game of who can take the biggest risk, or a way to "show off" how tough you are. It's not about being reckless, ignoring rules, or heading off alone just to prove something.

In fact, survival is often the opposite of danger—it's about recognizing risk and making smart choices to stay away from it.

So What Is Survival?

Survival is about being:

1. *Smart instead of showy*

2. *Calm instead of panicked*

3. *Careful instead of careless*

4. *Ready instead of reckless*

Let's bust a few myths:

❌ **Survival isn't about going out into the wild with nothing.**
Real survivors are prepared. They plan ahead. They pack smart. They let others know where they're going.

❌ **It's not about fighting nature.**
Nature isn't your enemy, it's your environment. A good survivor learns to observe, respect, and work with the natural world, not against it.

❌ **It's not about acting like a superhero.**
You don't need superpowers. You need calm thinking, good decisions, and confidence in the basics.

❌ **And it's definitely not about being alone.**
In real survival, asking for help and staying with your group are signs of strength, not weakness.

Survival Is for Everyone

You don't have to be an adult, a soldier, or a wilderness expert to learn survival skills.
You don't need a tent on your back or a firestarter in your pocket to get started.
You don't even need to leave your backyard.

Survival skills are for everyone, especially YOU.

If you're a kid who likes hiking, biking, or playing outdoors...
If you're someone who wants to feel brave instead of nervous when the weather changes...
If you've ever wondered, "What would I do if I got lost?"...
Then you're in the right place.

This book is made just for you.

Where Can You Use These Skills?
You'll be surprised how many places you can use survival thinking:

- On a hike with your family
- While camping at night under the stars
- If you get separated from your group at a park
- When a storm knocks out the power at home
- Even at school, if there's an emergency and you need to stay calm and help others

You don't need to be in the middle of nowhere. You just need to know what to do when things don't go as planned.

What If You're Not "Outdoorsy"?

That's okay! You don't have to love mud, bugs, or big forests to be a great problem-solver. You don't have to sleep in a tent or roast marshmallows to be prepared.

This book isn't just about forests. It's about confidence.
It's about understanding yourself.
It's about staying sharp, clear-headed, and safe—anytime, anywhere.

No matter your age, your experience, or your background, you can be a survival thinker.

Let's turn that spark inside you into a skill that lasts a lifetime.

What would you do

Now that you've started to learn what survival really means, it's time to put your brain to work.

Survival situations don't come with signs or step-by-step instructions. Sometimes, you have to think fast and make good choices. That's why every smart explorer needs to ask themselves: "What would I do if this happened to me?"

Read the three tricky situations given ahead. Don't rush. Read each one carefully, imagine yourself there, and think like a survivor.

Scenario 1: Lost on The Trail

You were walking with your hiking group, but now you can't see anyone. You try calling out, but no one answers. The trees all look the same. You feel your heart pounding.

What would you do?
Would you run and try to find them?
Would you panic and cry?
Or would you sit down, breathe deeply, and remember what you've learned?

The smart choice is to stay put. Getting more lost won't help. Sit down, stay calm, and listen. Help is more likely to find you if you don't wander off.

Scenario 2: Super Thirsty

You're on a nature walk and your water bottle is empty. You see a puddle nearby and it looks clean... kind of. The sun is hot, and your mouth is dry.

What would you do?
Would you drink the water right away?
Would you try to find a better source?
Would you remember what the book said about filtering and boiling water?

The truth is, even "clean" looking water can carry germs that make you sick. A true survival thinker doesn't take that risk. You'd look for running water, filter it through cloth if you had to, and wait to boil it if possible.

Scenario 3: A Cave in the Woods

You're exploring and see a big rocky cave in the hillside. It looks dry and kind of cool. You're curious. Should you go in and explore?

Wait—what if something is living in there? What if it's not safe?

A real survival thinker knows to stop and observe. You'd look for tracks, droppings, or strange smells. If anything feels off, you stay away. Your safety matters more than curiosity.

What Did You Learn?

Being brave doesn't mean charging ahead. It means thinking clearly, even when things get confusing. The best survivors ask themselves smart questions and trust their training.

Would you make the safe choice, or the fast one? Keep reading, and we'll keep building your survival brain.

You've got this!

Your Brain is Your SURVIVAL Superpower

What Does It Mean to Stay Calm?

When something goes wrong, your brain sounds an alarm. It tells your body to "do something, fast!" Your heart might race. Your hands might shake. You might feel like crying, yelling, or running. That's normal. It's your body trying to protect you from danger.

But here's the secret: that reaction can sometimes make things worse. When you're in a survival situation; lost in the woods, separated from your group, stuck in bad weather; what you do first can make all the difference.

Staying calm is the first and most important survival skill of all. Why? Because calm thinking helps you remember what to do. It helps you make smart decisions instead of panicked ones. It keeps your brain working, your breathing steady, and your body safe.

Survival isn't about being fearless. It's about knowing how to deal with fear when it shows up. Even the best explorers get scared. What makes them strong is that they know how to stop, breathe, and take control of their thoughts.

In this chapter, you'll learn how to do just that.

Why Panic Is the Real Danger

When something unexpected happens, it's normal to feel scared. But panic makes things worse. It makes your heart race, your thoughts scramble, and your body freeze or rush into danger.

Panic can make people:

Run in the wrong direction
Forget simple survival skills they already know
Ignore signs of danger
Take risks they wouldn't normally take

That's why the first survival skill every explorer learns is how to pause and breathe. Even when your heart is pounding, you can choose to slow down.

The Power of Pausing

Let's say you trip on a trail and fall behind your group. Your first instinct might be to run and yell. But what if instead, you stop? You breathe in through your nose and out through your mouth.
You tell yourself:
"I've read about this. I know what to do."

That moment of calm is when your survival skills can start to kick in.
You'll remember to:

→ Look for trail signs
→ Stay in one spot
→ Use your whistle
→ Make a plan

And guess what? Staying calm makes it easier for rescuers to find you.

S.T.O.P
Mindfulness Method

Here's a simple tool that survival experts use, and you can too. It's called the S.T.O.P. method, and it helps you think clearly in emergencies.

S STOP	Freeze. Don't keep walking. Don't yell. Just stop.
T THINK	Think about what happened, what do you know, are you really alone or just off-track.
O OBSERVE	Look and listen. Can you see trail markers? Hear voices? Is there shelter nearby?
P PLAN	Now that you've calmed down and looked around, what's the smartest next step? Should you stay put and wait? Use your whistle? Build a small shelter?

This method works in the woods, on a field trip, even in a city emergency. Stop. Think. Observe. Plan.

Remember, survivors don't always move first. They think first.

Real Life Mini Story
[Lucas & the Wrong Turn]

Lucas was 9 years old when he went hiking with his cousins at a state park. They had taken two different trails before, and Lucas thought he remembered which one was the right way. So when his cousins turned a corner and disappeared, Lucas followed... the wrong way. He didn't notice the quiet at first. But after a few minutes, he looked around and realized: he didn't recognize anything.

His stomach turned. His palms got sweaty. His thoughts started racing: What if I'm really lost? What if I never find them? Should I yell? Should I run?
But then something clicked.

He remembered reading a survival guide in school. It said:

"If you think you're lost, stop. Sit. Breathe."

Lucas sat on a rock. He drank some water. He took 3 deep breaths.
And then... he heard voices. Faintly. Behind him.
He stayed put. His cousin came back for him.
He didn't scream. He didn't run.

He stopped, and it worked.

What Would Panic Do Instead?

Let's go back to Lucas. He remembered what he had read, used the **S.T.O.P. method**, and stayed calm until his group found him. But what if he had panicked?

What if he had started running without thinking?
He might've gone deeper into the woods and ended up farther from the path.
What if he had started yelling and crying so loudly he couldn't hear his cousin calling for him?
He might have missed the very sound that could have led him back.
What if he had gotten so worked up that he forgot he had a water bottle, a map, or even his whistle?
Panic has a way of shrinking your memory. It makes you forget smart things you already know.

Panic doesn't just make you move fast. It makes you move without thinking. It tells you that you have to do something now, even when staying still is the smarter choice. It can cause you to rush into danger, ignore signs of safety, or lose energy too quickly.

That's why **it's important to practice calm** before something happens. The more often you practice stopping and thinking clearly, the easier it becomes, just like practicing a knot or using a compass. You're training your brain to be a great survival tool.

So ask yourself:
When something scary happens, who do I want to be. Lucas who stopped and thought, or the version of Lucas who panicked and got even more lost?

Practice Staying Calm

You don't have to wait for a real survival situation to learn how to stay calm, you can practice that skill right now, right where you are. The more you train your brain to handle stress when things are normal, the more it will know what to do when something unexpected happens.

Let's try it together.

Start by sitting still. Put your hands on your knees or in your lap. You don't have to close your eyes unless you want to. Just focus on what you feel.

Now take a slow, deep breath through your nose. Count to four as you do it.
1... 2... 3... 4...
Hold your breath for just a moment. Now breathe out slowly through your mouth.
4... 3... 2... 1...

Feel how your shoulders drop. Feel your heartbeat slow just a little. That's your body shifting from panic to peace. Now say this to yourself—quietly or out loud:

"I am okay. I know what to do. I can think clearly."
This is your calm zone. You can come here anytime; before a test, during a storm, or when you feel confused in the outdoors.

It only takes a few seconds, but it gives you something powerful: control. Great explorers don't just survive. They stay steady when the wind blows hardest. And now you know how to do that too.

Bonus Scenario – A Sudden Storm

You're halfway through a fun day hike with your family. The sun was shining when you left, but now dark clouds are creeping in. The wind picks up. The trees start to sway. You hear a deep rumble of thunder far off in the distance. You didn't pack your raincoat. You're not sure how far the parking lot is. The air feels tense. Your heart starts to beat faster.

What do you do?

Do you panic? Do you start running? Do you freeze in place and worry about being wet or cold? Or do you stop, breathe, and think?
Here's how a survival thinker handles it:

Stop.
Rushing could lead you off-trail. You need to stay steady.

Think.
You still have time to act smart before the storm hits.

Observe.
Look around. Do you see shelter nearby? A group of trees (but not tall, lonely ones)? A large rock outcrop to sit near?

Plan.
Move calmly to the safest, lowest, and most covered place you can find (not a cave).

Crouch low on your backpack (not flat on the ground), keep your head down, and wait it out. Rain doesn't last forever. But panic can lead to poor decisions that last longer.

A real storm doesn't just test your gear, it tests your mind. And you've been practicing that. When you stay calm in a storm, you don't just survive, you grow stronger.
So next time the wind picks up or the sky turns dark, you'll know exactly what to do:

Pause. Breathe. Think. And move wisely.

Reflection Journal

Survival isn't just about what you do. It's also about how you think and learn. Every experience you have, every challenge you face, and every time you choose calm over panic... you grow.

These journal pages are your space to stop, reflect, and explore what's going on inside your survival brain. The more you understand yourself, the more prepared you'll be in the real world.

Take your time. There are no wrong answers, only honest ones.

1. What does your body feel like when you get nervous or scared?

(Do your hands get sweaty? Does your heart race? Do you feel frozen?)

2. What is one thing that helps you calm down when you feel that way?

(Deep breaths? A safe place? A kind thought?)

3. Think of a time when something went wrong.
Did you stay calm? Did you panic? What did you learn from that moment?

4. Imagine you're in the woods and get turned around.
What would you want your brain to say to you in that moment?
Write down a message you could repeat to yourself.

5. What does "staying calm" mean to you in your everyday life?

(Hint: it might be during school, arguments, storms, or when you're nervous)

This page is a tool, just like your compass or your water bottle. Use it to check in with your best survival skill: your thinking.

Great explorers are great reflectors.

Calm Superpowers Badge

You've just finished one of the most powerful chapters in this book. You've learned how to control the storm inside you.

You now have the ability to pause when others rush. To breathe when things get loud. To think when panic tries to take over. That's a superpower.

And guess what? You've earned your first badge!

CALM SUPERPOWERS

CALM SUPERPOWERS

Below is your Calm Superpowers Checklist. Read each line and place a ✅ next to the ones that feel true for you today. (You can always come back and check more later.)

My Calm Superpowers

□ I know how to stop and take a deep breath before reacting

□ I understand how panic affects my body and mind

□ I can sit still, listen, and think clearly under pressure

□ I know the S.T.O.P. method and when to use it

□ I trust myself to stay calm when things go wrong

□ I can lead others by staying grounded and steady

□ I've practiced calming down even when things are fine

□ I know that survival is about thinking, not rushing

Finding Safe Shelter
Where to Go, Where Not to Go

Shelter = Safety

When you think of survival, what's the first thing that comes to mind? Food? Water? Fire?

Those are all important, but when you're stuck in the outdoors, shelter is often what you need first.

Why?

Because your body can handle being hungry for a while. It can even go without water for a short time. But exposure—to cold, rain, wind, or sun—can make you weak, sick, or even dangerously dehydrated.

That's why finding shelter is one of the first things you should do when you're lost, waiting to be found, or staying put during an emergency.

Shelter keeps you dry.
Shelter keeps you warm.
Shelter keeps you safe.

It can be natural (like a rock overhang or a thicket of trees), or something you build yourself with your surroundings.

This chapter will show you how to think like a shelter-builder, and how to pick the right spot to rest, wait, and stay protected.

Where NOT to Build a Shelter

Before you grab branches and start building, there's something even more important to know:

The wrong place to build a shelter can be more dangerous than having no shelter at all.
That's why smart survivors always look around and ask, "Is this spot safe?" before doing anything.

Let's look at places to avoid when choosing where to rest or build a shelter:

❌ **Near Water** ❌

Streams, rivers, or dry creek beds might look peaceful—but during storms, they can flood fast. Even if the ground looks dry, rain upstream can send water rushing through in minutes.

Avoid:

- Sleeping right next to rivers or lakes
- Camping in low areas with smooth rocks or washed-out soil
- Creek beds (even dry ones!)

❌ Under Tall, Lonely Trees❌

If it's raining or storming, big tall trees can attract lightning. If it's windy, those same trees can drop branches.

Avoid:

- The tallest tree in a clearing
- Trees with broken limbs above you
- "Widow-makers" (dead branches hanging overhead)

❌ On Steep Hills or Cliffs❌

It might feel exciting to be on a hilltop, but those places are exposed to wind, cold, and danger from slipping.

Avoid:

- Loose slopes with rocks
- Edges of cliffs or sharp drop-offs
- Areas where rain might cause mudslides

❌ Near Animal Trails or Burrows❌

It might feel exciting to be on a hilltop, but those places are exposed to wind, cold, and danger from slipping.

Avoid:

- Loose slopes with rocks
- Edges of cliffs or sharp drop-offs
- Areas where rain might cause mudslides

❌ In Wet, Low, or Mushy Areas❌

If the ground feels spongy or soft, it's probably not a good place to build. It'll make you cold, wet, and uncomfortable in no time.

Avoid:

- Muddy patches
- Spots where water pools after rain
- Deep shady dips with no sunlight

The Best Places to Find or Build Shelter

Now that you know where not to build a shelter, let's talk about where you should go when you need protection from the weather.

The best shelter spots are places that help you feel safe, dry, and calm—places where you can think clearly and plan your next move.

Here are some smart survival-tested locations to look for:

✅ In a Natural Hollow or Dip (But Not Too Low)✅

Look for gently sloped ground, not deep valleys or wet ditches. A small rise nearby can block the wind, and soft leaves make better insulation than bare dirt.

Try to find:

- A spot that's above low flood zones, but not on a windy hilltop
- Ground with leaves, pine needles, or dry grass
- A place that feels tucked in, but not trapped

✅ Near (But Not Next To) Water ✅

Water is important for survival, but you don't want to be too close. Choose a spot where you can see or hear water, but you're still 15–20 steps away from the edge.

Why? Because that protects you from:

- Flash floods
- Cold damp ground
- Mosquitoes or animal visitors

✅ Behind a Wind Block ✅

Survivors learn to work with nature. A large rock, a downed tree, or a group of thick bushes can block wind and even reflect your body heat back toward you.

Bonus: If you use one of these as a wall, you only need to build one side of your shelter!

Look for:

- Rock faces with overhangs
- Clusters of low trees
- Fallen logs with space behind them

✅ In a Spot You Can Be Seen (Eventually) ✅

If you're waiting for help, don't hide your shelter too well. Choose a spot that gives you protection and a clear area nearby where rescuers might spot you.

Survival is about staying safe and being smart about being found.

Remember: The best shelters work with the land, not against it. Use what nature gives you, think like a builder, and stay dry, warm, and aware of your surroundings.

How to Build a Lean-To Shelter

Sometimes there's no perfect rock wall, bush, or dry cave nearby. That's okay—because you can build your own shelter using branches, leaves, and a little creativity.

One of the simplest and smartest survival shelters is called a lean-to. It's easy to build, works well in wind or rain, and uses things you can usually find in the woods.

Let's learn how to make one, step by step.

What You'll Need:

1 long, sturdy branch (at least as tall as you are)
A big rock, tree stump, or log to lean it against
Lots of smaller branches or sticks (as long as your arms)
A pile of dry leaves, pine needles, grass, or bark
Rope, string, or shoelaces (optional, but helpful)

Step 1: Set Up Your Frame

Find a tree or a big rock. Lean your longest branch against it so that it makes a slanted roof shape. This branch is called your ridgepole—it's the backbone of your shelter.

Make sure the slant isn't too steep or too flat. Just enough for rain to slide off.

Step 2: Build the Walls

Place smaller sticks and branches against the ridgepole like ribs. Start from the bottom and lean them upward, side by side, like the slats of a fence.

Leave just enough space at one end for a small entrance.

Step 3: Insulate

Now cover everything with leaves, grass, pine needles, or bark. You want the walls to be thick—at least as thick as your arm. This helps keep wind out and warmth in.

Pack some dry leaves inside too, like a mattress or blanket. The ground steals your body heat, so extra padding helps you stay warm.

Step 4: Test It Out

Crawl inside. Can you sit or lie down without getting wet? Can wind blow through the walls? Do you feel cozy and protected?

If yes, congrats! You've made a real shelter.
If not, add more leaves or fix the gaps. Problem-solving is part of the fun.

Remember: your shelter doesn't have to be perfect. It just has to keep you safe, dry, and calm until help arrives or the weather passes.

Other Types of Survival Shelters

The lean-to is just one way to stay safe in the wild—but it's not the only option! Different weather, terrain, and materials can call for different kinds of shelters. The best survivors know how to look at their surroundings and choose the right kind of cover for the moment.

Let's explore three other kid-friendly shelter types that are simple, smart, and effective when built carefully.

1. The A-Frame Shelter

This is like a double-sided lean-to, shaped like an upside-down "V" or the roof of a house.

How to make it:

- Lean two long branches against a log or tree at an angle, so they touch at the top
- Fill in both sides with ribs (smaller sticks)
- Cover both sides with leaves or grass
- Leave a small gap for the entrance

Why it works:

Great wind protection from both sides. Best for cold nights or open areas where wind changes direction.

2. The Debris Hut

This one is great for staying warm.

How to make it:

Find a thick branch and lean it on a stump or forked stick

Build a frame around it using ribs, like a tiny triangle tunnel

Cover the entire thing with a HUGE pile of leaves, grass, and bark

Crawl in through a small opening (just enough to squeeze in)

Why it works:

Super warm! It traps your body heat inside. Best for cold, windy weather—but not great for long stays.

3. The Tarp Shelter (If You Have Gear)

This one is great for staying warm.

How to make it:

Find a thick branch and lean it on a stump or forked stick
Build a frame around it using ribs, like a tiny triangle tunnel
Cover the entire thing with a HUGE pile of leaves, grass, and bark
Crawl in through a small opening (just enough to squeeze in)

Why it works:

Super warm! It traps your body heat inside. Best for cold, windy weather—but not great for long stays.

Tools That Help You Build Like a Pro

Great shelter-builders don't just use their hands—they use smart tools that make their shelters stronger, faster, and safer to build. Some tools are found in nature, and some come in your survival kit.

You don't need a giant toolbox or sharp gadgets to be a pro. You just need the right items and the wisdom to use them carefully.

Let's go through the most helpful shelter-building tools for kids—and how to use them wisely.

Rope or Paracord

Rope is like magic in the wild. You can use it to:

- Tie sticks together for stability
- Secure a tarp between trees
- Strengthen the frame of your shelter
- Create pegs and guy lines for wind protection

Pro Tip: Always carry rope or paracord in your survival kit. It's light and has so many uses.

Pocket Knife (Supervised Use)

A small, foldable knife can help:

- Sharpen sticks
- Trim rope
- Cut bark for cord
- Shape wooden pegs

Rule #1: Never use a knife unless an adult has trained you—and always use it with care.

A Tarp or Emergency Blanket

A plastic tarp or reflective emergency blanket can turn a simple stick frame into a weatherproof shelter in seconds.

You can:

- Drape it over a ridgepole like a roof
- Use it to line the floor
- Turn it into a water catcher

Pro Tip: Bright-colored tarps can also help rescuers spot you faster.

Big Leaves, Bark, and Grass

Nature gives you building supplies too. Use:

Palm leaves or ferns for a rain roof

Bark slabs as panels

Dry grass or pine needles for insulation

Survivors look around and think: What can I use that's already here?

Your Backpack

Wait—your backpack? Yup! It's not just for carrying things.

You can use it as:

A wind blocker behind your body

A cushion for sitting or crouching

A weight to help hold down tarp corners

A shield while collecting branches

Why Water Matters Most

You can survive without food for a while. You can last without shelter, even in tough weather. But without water? Your body starts to slow down fast.

Water keeps you strong.
Water keeps your brain sharp.
Water keeps your body working the way it's supposed to.

Even just one day without drinking enough water can make you feel dizzy, tired, confused, and sick. That's why learning how to find and drink safe water is one of the most important survival skills of all.

But wait, just because you see water in nature doesn't mean it's safe to drink. Some water can make you even more sick if it has bacteria, dirt, or chemicals in it.

This chapter will teach you:

- *How to know when water is safe*
- *Where to look for it in the wild*
- *How to clean it if you have to drink it*
- *And what never to drink, no matter how thirsty you are*

Before you learn how to start a fire or build a shelter, this might just be the thing that saves your life someday.

Because smart survivors don't just find water.
They think before they drink.

Where to Look for Water in the Wild

When you're outdoors without a water bottle, knowing where to look for natural water could make the difference between staying strong or getting weak. Here's how smart survivors find water in the wild:

---

1. Streams, Creeks, and Rivers

These are your best bet in the wild. Flowing water is usually cleaner because it moves, which means bacteria and dirt don't have time to sit and grow. Look for clear, fast-moving water. If it's rushing over rocks or downhill, that's a good sign. Still, it's best to treat the water before drinking just to be safe.
Avoid: water that smells bad, looks slimy, has foam or bubbles, or is filled with bugs or algae.

2. Lakes and Ponds

If you can't find a stream or river, a lake or pond is the next option. But be careful—because the water doesn't move, it's easier for germs and bugs to grow. That means you should always clean this kind of water before drinking it, no matter how clear it looks.
Check the edges. If animals are drinking from it, and it smells okay, it might be usable, but only after you purify it.

3. Rainwater

Rain is one of the cleanest sources of water in nature—as long as you collect it the right way. Use whatever you have: a cup, a pot, a poncho, a tarp, or even leaves shaped into a bowl. Try to catch rain directly from the sky, not off rooftops or dirty surfaces.

This is one of the safest ways to get drinkable water outdoors.

4. Morning Dew

In the early morning, grass and leaves are often covered in dew—tiny drops of water from overnight air. You can wipe this up with a clean cloth, T-shirt, or bandana, then wring it into a container or your mouth.

It takes time, and you won't get much, but it's better than nothing if you're desperate.

5. Plants and Vines

Some plants store water inside their stems. Grape vines, for example, can be cut and tipped downward to drip out liquid. Bamboo and some thick-leaved plants may hold moisture too.

Important: Never try this unless you know the plant is safe. Some vines and plants can be poisonous. If you're not 100% sure, don't risk it.

6. Animal Trails

Animals need water too. If you see a lot of animal tracks or a trail through the grass, it might lead to a stream or pond. Birds flying low in the early morning or insects swarming in one direction can also be clues.

Just be careful—don't follow animals too closely or walk into places that feel unsafe or unfamiliar.

<u>*Important Reminder:*</u>

Even if water looks clean, that doesn't mean it is clean. Bacteria, parasites, and chemicals can be invisible. That's why the next step is learning how to clean water before drinking it.

How to Make Water Safe to Drink

Finding water is just the first step. The next, and maybe most important step is making sure that water is safe to drink.

Even water that looks clean can still contain germs, parasites, or chemicals that can make you sick. You can't always see what's in water, so smart survivors always treat water before drinking it, just to be safe.

Here are several ways to make wild water safer:

1. Boil It

Boiling is the best way to kill bacteria and parasites. If you have a pot and a way to make fire, bring the water to a rolling boil for at least 1 full minute. Let it cool before drinking.

If you're at a higher altitude (like in the mountains), boil it for at least 3 minutes instead.

2. Use Purification Tablets

Survival kits often include water purification tablets. These little tablets contain chemicals that kill germs in water. Just follow the instructions on the packet; usually, you drop one tablet into your water container, shake it, and wait 30–60 minutes.

These tablets are light, small, and easy to carry, which makes them a great tool to include in a survival bag.

3. Filter It

You can use a water filter straw or bottle, which is designed to trap bacteria and dirt before the water reaches your mouth. These filters are common in hiking stores and are a great option for emergencies.

If you don't have one, you can make a basic filter by:

- Using a clean cloth, bandana, or shirt to strain out dirt and leaves
- Pouring the water through a homemade filter made from sand, charcoal, and gravel layered in a plastic bottle (this removes debris but not all germs)

Even filtered water should still be boiled or treated if possible.

4. Use UV Light (Advanced)

Some survival tools use ultraviolet light to kill bacteria. These devices look like a pen and shine UV rays into the water. They work well—but they require batteries and aren't as common.

If you don't have one, focus on boiling or using tablets instead.

Never Drink Water That:

- *Has foam, oil, or scum on the surface*
- *Smells like chemicals or rotten eggs*
- *Comes from a swamp, ditch, or puddle*
- *Is near animal waste or dead animals*
- *Looks green, cloudy, or bright-colored*

Survivor's Rule:

If you're not sure it's safe, don't drink it. It's better to wait and treat it than to risk getting sick in the wild.

Read the next page to learn what never to drink, even if you're really, really thirsty.

What Never to Drink, No Matter How Thirsty You Are!

When you're hot, tired, and thirsty, almost any water can start to look good. But in survival situations, drinking the wrong kind of water can make you very sick—even faster than not drinking at all.
Here's a list of water sources you should never drink, even if you're really thirsty:

1. Puddles or Ditches
Puddles may look harmless, but they often contain oil, dirt, chemicals, or germs. Water that's been sitting on the ground can grow bacteria quickly, especially near roads or trails.

2. Swamps or Marshes
Swamp water is usually still, green, and full of bacteria and insects. It often smells bad and may be full of things you can't see: parasites, algae, or waste from animals. Even filtering it might not make it safe enough.

3. Water Near Dead Animals or Waste
If you see a dead animal near the water, or signs of poop or waste around it, stay away. That water could be full of dangerous bacteria that can make you sick fast.

4. Salt Water (Ocean Water)
Even though oceans are huge and full of water, you can't drink it. Salt water dehydrates you, which means it makes your body lose water instead of gain it. Drinking it will only make you thirstier, and sicker.

5. Bright Green or Colored Water

Water that's bright green, red, or cloudy might have algae or chemical pollution in it. If the water looks like a strange color or has stuff floating in it, do not drink it.

6. Water That Smells Bad

If water smells like rotten eggs, garbage, gasoline, or anything chemical, don't even touch it. Water should be clear, calm-smelling, and natural. A bad smell is a strong warning sign.

7. Snow or Ice (Without Melting It First)

You can drink melted snow or ice, but don't eat it directly. It lowers your body temperature, which can make it harder to stay warm. If you need to use snow, melt it first in a container or by holding it near your body before drinking.

Important Rule:

If it looks weird, smells weird, or sits still, don't drink it. Just a few sips of bad water can lead to cramps, vomiting, or diarrhea, and those make it even harder to survive.

How to Carry and Store Water the Smart Way

Finding water is only half the job. Once you've collected it and cleaned it, you need to make sure it stays safe until you drink it.

In the wild, water can get dirty again if you're not careful. A clean stream or a filtered bottle doesn't help much if your container leaks, your lid is dirty, or you forget which bottle has clean water and which one doesn't.

That's why every smart survivor learns how to carry water without spilling it, store it without contamination, and tell clean water from dirty water at a glance.

Let's go over the best ways to do all three.

1. Always Use the Cleanest Container You Can Find
If you have a water bottle or canteen, great! Make sure it's washed out before using it. If you're using something like a cup, jar, or plastic bag, rinse it with clean water first if possible.

<u>Don't use containers that:</u>

- Smell like soap, fuel, or chemicals
- Have leftover food or sticky stuff inside
- Are covered in dirt, mold, or slime

Why it matters: Even one drop of something toxic can make your clean water dangerous to drink.

2. Cover Your Water
Once you've collected water, always cover the container. You can use:

- A lid (best option)
- A clean cloth tied over the top
- A flat rock or large leaf if that's all you have

This helps keep out:
- Dirt and dust from the wind
- Falling leaves, insects, and bird droppings
- Germs from your hands or nearby gear

Think of your water like food. If you wouldn't eat food off the forest floor, don't let your water stay open to the air too long.

3. Carry It Securely

If you're walking, your water needs to come with you. Tuck your bottle into your pack, or tie it on with rope, string, or paracord. If it's open-topped, walk slowly and hold it upright.

Bonus tip: If you're using a bag or soft container, double-check for leaks. A slow drip could waste all your water without you even noticing.

4. Don't Mix Clean and Dirty Water

This one's important: if you're carrying untreated water (water you haven't boiled or purified yet), don't mix it with your clean supply.

Keep a system:
- Wrap a string or bandana around the "dirty" container
- Mark it with an "X" using charcoal or a stick
- Store dirty and clean water on opposite sides of your bag

5. Keep It Out of the Sun

Sunlight can heat your water quickly. If your container is see-through and sits in the sun, bacteria can grow faster, especially if the water wasn't treated well in the first place.

Best practice: Keep your water in the shade and drink it within 12 to 24 hours.

6. Make a Simple Water Kit

A good survivor is always prepared. Keep a small water-carrying kit in your pack with:

- A plastic bottle or collapsible container
- A bandana for filtering
- A zip-top bag for collecting rain or dew
- A tiny cup for dipping or drinking
- A marker or string for labeling clean vs. untreated water
-

It doesn't have to be fancy, just smart.

Because when it comes to water, it's not just what you find.
It's **how you protect it** that keeps you safe.

What to Do If You Can't Find Water Anywhere

Sometimes, even when you've searched carefully, you might not find any water right away. Maybe it hasn't rained in a while. Maybe there's no stream, no pond, no puddle, not even a patch of dew.

Don't panic.

This page is about what to do when water isn't easy to find—but you still need to think smart, stay calm, and stretch your energy until you can find it again.

Step 1: Stop Moving and Conserve Energy

The more you move, the more you sweat. And the more you sweat, the faster your body loses water.
So the first thing to do is slow down.

Find a shady spot. Sit or lie down. Keep cool. This helps your body hold on to moisture for as long as possible.

Important: Never walk in the heat of the day if you don't have water. If you need to travel, wait until early morning or late evening.

Step 2: Check for Hidden Water Sources

Look again, but more carefully this time.
Try:

- Digging a small hole near green plants or in a dry stream bed
- Turning over rocks in the morning to look for condensation

- Watching birds and animals for movement toward water
- Searching under tree roots or low areas for damp ground

Even **a little water** is better than none. Be patient. Think like a tracker.

Step 3: Collect Moisture from the Air

Even if you can't find a stream or pond, you can still collect tiny amounts of water from the air.

Try:

- Tying a clean cloth around your ankle and walking through tall grass in the early morning, then wringing it out
- Spreading out a plastic bag, tarp, or poncho at night to catch dew
- Using a solar still (we'll cover that in a later section)

It might not fill your bottle, but it can keep your mouth moist and your body going.

Step 4: Avoid Foods That Dry You Out

If you don't have water, don't eat salty or dry foods like trail mix, crackers, or jerky.

Eating without water makes digestion harder—and that makes you even more thirsty.

Survivor tip: If you're very thirsty and have no water, it's better to skip food altogether until you've rehydrated.

Step 5: Stay Calm and Make a Plan

Running around looking for water in every direction will only make things worse. Sit down.

Ask yourself:

- Where have I already checked?
- Are there signs of animals, bugs, or birds nearby?
- Do I remember any streams or puddles from earlier?

You don't need to find a lake, you just need enough to keep going.

Reminder:

Your Body Can Survive a Day or Two Without Water
It's not ideal, but it's possible.
Don't panic if you haven't found any yet.

Instead, slow down, think clearly, and look with focus.
Smart survivors don't give up.

They problem solve, even when things feel tough.

How to Make a Solar Still (A Water Collector Made from the Sun!)

When there's no stream, no pond, and no rain in sight, there's still one amazing tool you can use to get water: the sun.

A solar still is a simple setup that uses the sun's heat to turn moisture from the ground or plants into drinkable water. It might not give you a full bottle, but even a few drops can help you stay hydrated.

Here's how it works, and how you can build one if you ever need it.

What You'll Need:

- A plastic sheet, clear or see-through (like a zip-top bag, plastic wrap, or emergency poncho)
- A container (like a cup, can, bottle top, or clean bowl)
- A small rock or weight
- A shovel or digging stick

How to Build a Solar Still:

<u>Step 1: Pick a Good Spot</u>
Find a place where the ground is damp, like:

- A dry stream bed
- Near plants or tree roots
- Any shady spot where morning dew was present

If there's no damp ground, you can put green leaves or grass in the hole. These release moisture when heated by the sun.

Step 2: Dig a Hole

Use your hands, a rock, or a stick to dig a bowl-shaped hole in the ground, about 2 feet wide and 1 foot deep.

Place your container in the center of the hole. Make sure it sits flat and steady.

Step 3: Cover the Hole with Plastic

Stretch the plastic sheet across the hole and secure the edges with rocks or dirt so no air can escape.

Then, place a small rock right in the center of the plastic, over the container. This should make the plastic dip slightly like a shallow cone, pointing down toward your cup.

Step 4: Let the Sun Do the Work

As the sun heats the ground, moisture will rise, hit the plastic, and drip down into the container. This water is clean, because it's been condensed from vapor.

Important: Don't let the plastic touch the container. If it does, the water may not drip inside.

How Much Water Will You Get?

A solar still won't give you a lot of water fast—maybe a few ounces in a full day. But in an emergency, every drop counts.

You can build more than one to increase your chances of staying hydrated.

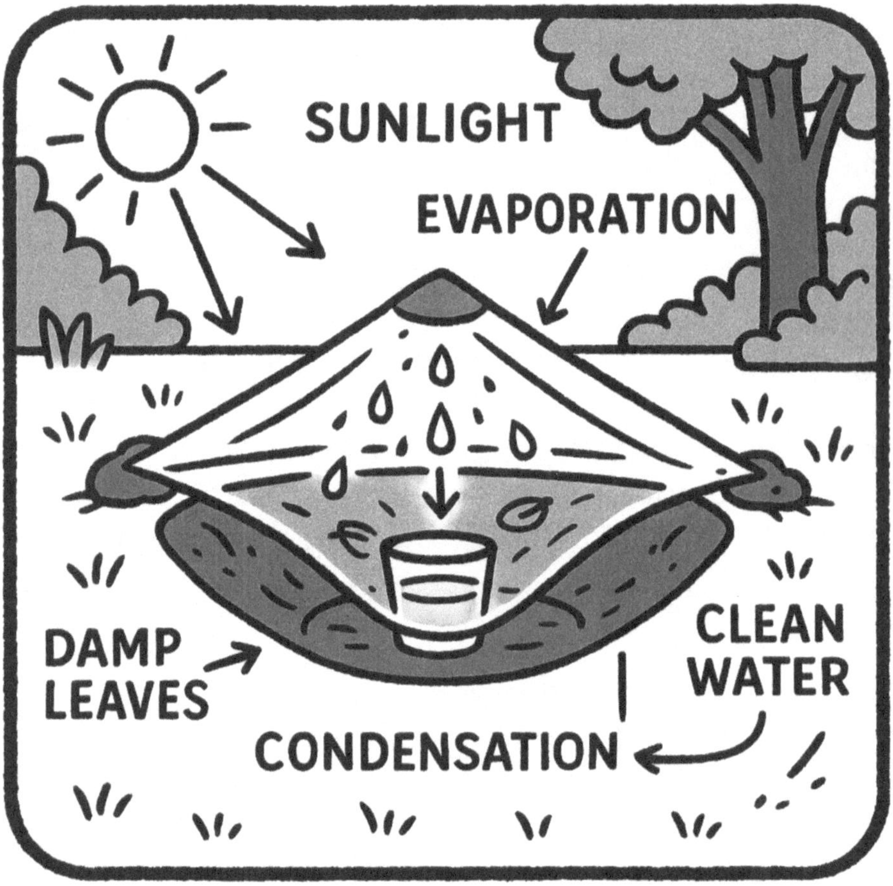

A Solar Still

Survival Reminder:
It might take time, but a solar still can mean the difference between getting weaker and staying strong.

When nature gives you sun and soil, a smart survivor turns them into water.

What to Pack in a Personal Survival Kit

When you're out exploring nature, one of the smartest things you can bring is a personal survival kit. It's small enough to carry in a backpack, but powerful enough to help you stay safe, warm, and prepared for the unexpected.

A good survival kit doesn't need to be fancy. It just needs to be filled with smart, useful tools; things that help you solve problems when you're away from home.
Let's break it down into the essentials.

The Basics (Every Kit Should Have These)

Whistle: For signaling if you're lost
Flashlight or glow stick: For light when it gets dark
Water bottle: Always stay hydrated
Bandana or cloth: Can be used as a filter, bandage, sun shield, or sling
Snacks: High-energy food like granola bars or trail mix
Map and compass: Old-school tools that don't need batteries
Small first-aid kit: Bandages, wipes, and gauze
Plastic bag or poncho: Can be used for rain cover or to catch water
Rope or string: Great for tying, building, or hanging gear
Pencil and notepad: To sketch maps or leave messages

Why These Items Matter

Each tool in your kit has more than one use. A flashlight isn't just for seeing, it can signal rescuers. A bandana can cover your head, act as a water filter, or be tied as a tourniquet.

Bonus Items (If You Have Space)

- Fire starter (with adult permission and supervision)
- Emergency blanket (reflects heat and folds small)
- Mirror or shiny object for signaling
- Glow-in-the-dark stickers to mark gear at night
- Extra shoelaces or cord for repairs or shelter

Try This

Make your own kit at home! Lay everything out and pack it in a pouch or zip-top bag. Then ask yourself:

- Can I carry this all day?
- Do I know how to use each item?
- What else would I add based on where I live?

Survival doesn't start in the wild. It starts with preparation, and your kit is a great place to begin.

How to Signal for Help (So You Can Be Found Faster!)

Getting found is just as important as staying calm. When you're lost or stuck in the wild, sitting and waiting isn't enough, you have to help rescuers find you.

This is where signaling comes in. **Signaling means using tools, sounds, or shapes to get attention and let people know where you are.**

There are three main ways to signal for help:

1. Sound (they hear you)
2. Visual (they see you)
3. Ground signals (they recognize your message from above)

Sound Signals

Sound is one of the best tools you can use, especially if trees or fog block someone's view. Sound can travel through the forest, around corners, and even in the dark.

✅ **Use a whistle**

If you have a whistle, it's the most effective sound tool. Blow three short blasts; this is the universal distress signal. Wait 30 seconds, then do it again.

A whistle is louder than your voice and doesn't wear you out. If someone's nearby, this pattern helps them recognize that you're signaling, not just making noise by accident.

✅ **If you don't have a whistle**

You can still make sounds with natural materials. Try:

- Banging two rocks together
- Tapping a stick against a hollow log or tree
- Clanging a metal pot, cup, or spoon

Whatever you use, do it in a steady, repeated rhythm. Natural sounds (like wind or animals) are random. Repeated tapping or clanging tells rescuers, "A person is here!"

⚠️ **Shouting is the last resort**

Yelling drains your energy and dries your throat. It also doesn't travel very far, especially in windy or wooded areas. Use it only if you hear voices nearby or have no other option.

Visual Signals

Visual signals are how you stand out from your surroundings. If someone is looking for you from far away on foot, by drone, or from a helicopter, what will they see?

✅ **Use bright colors**

Nature is mostly green and brown. A red, orange, or neon yellow jacket or backpack pops out immediately. Lay it flat on the ground in an open space.

You can also wave it from a high spot or hang it from a stick like a flag.

The bigger the item, the better. Spread it out so it's visible from a distance.

✅ **Use light**

If you have something shiny, like:

- A mirror
- A metal spoon or phone screen
- A compact or flashlight

You can use it to reflect sunlight toward a distant person or aircraft. Turn the shiny surface back and forth in the direction of your target to send flashes of light.

At night, flashlights and headlamps are excellent. Flash the light three times in a row, wait, and repeat.

A steady beam is helpful, but pulses or flashes are easier to notice and can be recognized as a signal.

✅ **Make smoke (if you've built a fire)**

During the day, smoke can rise above the trees and be seen from far away. Use green leaves or damp grass to make the smoke thick and white or gray.

Just make sure the fire is under control and you have a safe spot cleared around it.

Smoke during the day and glowing flames at night can help rescuers locate you quickly.

Ground Signals

If someone is flying above or looking from a ridge, you can send a message without saying a word. Use the ground like a giant piece of paper, and draw with whatever you have.

✅ **Use natural materials**
Grab sticks, rocks, logs, leaves, or your gear and lay them out in big shapes in an open area. Your message should be simple, big, and bold, not something that blends in.

Try to make each letter or symbol as long as your whole body or even bigger.

✅ **The best symbols to use:**
SOS — the international distress code
X — means "I need help"
→ — an arrow pointing to where you've gone
HELP — the clearest message of all

Be sure to use contrast; dark objects on light dirt or sand, light-colored objects on dark soil or leaves. The easier it is to see, the faster you'll be found.

Once you've made your ground signal, stay close to it. If you wander away, rescuers might see your message but miss you entirely.

Final Tips:

- Use more than one signal if you can: sound + light, or ground + whistle
- Make your signals big, bold, and obvious
- Repeat your signals throughout the day
- Don't give up. People are looking for you

How to Stay Safe at Night in the Wild

Nighttime in the wild can feel spooky, but it doesn't have to be scary. The key to staying safe is staying calm, prepared, and smart about your surroundings.

Once the sun goes down, it's harder to see, harder to move around, and much easier to get lost or injured. That's why your best move at night is to stay in one place and settle in.

Let's break down exactly what to do when night falls:

1. Stay Put
If you're lost, it's almost always safer to stop moving after dark. Even with a flashlight, it's harder to see holes, roots, cliffs, or animals at night. Staying in one spot helps:

- Rescuers find you faster
- You avoid getting more lost or hurt
- You save energy and stay calm

Choose your resting spot before it gets completely dark. If you haven't already built a shelter, now's the time.

2. Choose a Safe Sleeping Spot
Look for a space that is:

- Flat and dry
- Not under dead branches or cliffs
- Away from rivers or streams (but not too far from your last water source)
- Sheltered from wind (like near a rock wall or cluster of bushes)

Clear away sticks, bugs, and sharp rocks before you lie down. If possible, build a small lean-to or debris shelter to keep warm.

3. Build a Small Fire (If Safe)
A small, well-built fire does three important things:

- Keeps you warm
- Scares off animals
- Gives you light and comfort

Only build a fire if:

- You know how to do it safely
- You've cleared space around it
- You have a way to put it out later

If you can't build a fire, use dry leaves, grass, or extra clothes to stay warm. You can also stuff your clothes with crumpled leaves for insulation.

4. Keep a Light Source Handy
If you have a flashlight, headlamp, or glow stick, keep it right next to you. Don't waste the batteries by keeping it on all night. Just use it when needed.

Flashing your light in **three quick bursts** every once in a while can help searchers spot you.

5. Don't Worry About Wild Animals
Most wild animals are more afraid of you than you are of them. Stay calm, stay quiet, and don't leave food out in the open.

You can tie your food in a bag and hang it from a tree branch a few feet off the ground and away from your shelter.

6. Get Some Rest

Even if you're nervous, your body needs rest to stay sharp. You might not sleep deeply, but closing your eyes, breathing slowly, and lying still can help recharge your energy.

Try this calming phrase:
"I'm safe. I'm strong. I'm smart. I'm okay."
Say it quietly to yourself while taking deep breaths.

Final Tip:
Night doesn't last forever.
You just need to stay calm, stay warm, and stay put until morning.

When the sun comes up, everything feels clearer—and you'll be ready for your next smart move.

How to Deal with Fear in the Wild

Everyone feels fear, even survival experts. When you're lost, alone, or facing something unfamiliar in nature, fear is your brain's way of saying, "Be careful!"

It's not something to be ashamed of. Fear is natural. It's part of how your body keeps you safe. It makes you alert. It gets your attention. It tells you to slow down and pay attention to your surroundings.

But fear can also grow fast, especially when you're tired, cold, or unsure what to do next. If you let fear take over, it can become panic, and **panic is what causes people to rush, get hurt, or make dangerous mistakes.**

Your heart might beat faster. Your hands might shake. Your mind might say things like, "What if I can't do this?" or "What if nobody finds me?"

That's why the smartest survivors don't try to be fearless. They know that **being brave doesn't mean you don't feel scared.** It means you learn how to feel scared and still keep your head.

They learn how to feel fear without freezing.
How to think clearly even when their heart is pounding.
How to take one small step instead of panicking or giving up.

You can learn that too.

Here's how.

Step 1: Name the Feeling
Start by saying it:
"I feel scared right now."

When you name fear, you shrink it. Instead of fear being this big cloud hanging over you, it becomes something you can see, and handle. You're not pretending it's not there. You're simply taking charge of it.

Step 2: Know What Fear Does to Your Body
Fear sends your body into "emergency mode." That's useful if you're running from danger, but not if you're just trying to think clearly.

Fear might make you:

- Breathe fast
- Sweat
- Shake
- Feel frozen or restless
- Imagine the worst
-

Knowing these are just body signals helps you realize:
"This is normal. My body is reacting, but I'm still in control."

Step 3: Breathe to Regain Control
Breathing is your number one tool to take charge again.
Try this simple technique:

- Inhale slowly through your nose for 4 seconds
- Hold it for 2 seconds
- Exhale slowly through your mouth for 6 seconds

Do this 3–5 times.

It helps slow your heart rate, calm your nerves, and clear your thinking. You'll feel your body start to shift back into "okay" mode.

Step 4: Focus on What's Real

Fear makes you think about what might happen. But survival thinking needs you to focus on what's real, right now.

Use your senses:

- **Look** around and name 5 things you can see
- **Listen** for 3 different sounds
- **Touch** 2 nearby objects; like your shoe, a rock, or a leaf

This tells your brain, "I'm here. I'm safe enough. I'm thinking clearly."

Step 5: Do One Small Thing

Now that you're calmer, give your brain a job:

- Organize your pack
- Check your shelter
- Gather a few sticks
- Adjust your map or compass
- Sit and plan your next signal

Doing something; anything helpful, gives you a sense of control, and that shrinks fear even more.

Even doing just one small thing, like straightening your shelter or picking up sticks for a signal can shift your focus from fear to action. That movement, that tiny decision, tells your brain, "I'm not stuck. I'm doing something."

And sometimes, doing something is all it takes to feel like you're back in charge. It doesn't have to be big. It just has to be intentional.

Survival isn't always about big hero moments.

Often, it's just about thinking clearly when your body wants to panic.

It's about taking a breath, calming your heart, and making the next smart move.

That's real strength, the kind that builds from the inside out.

Final Reminder:
Fear isn't the enemy.
It's a signal that you care about what happens next.
You can feel afraid and still:
Stay calm
Make good choices
Keep yourself safe
Be proud of how you handled it
That's what real survival heroes do.

What to Do If You're Hurt and You're Alone

Getting hurt in the wild can feel scary, especially if no one else is around. But injuries don't always mean danger. Many times, you can take care of yourself until help arrives or until you're strong enough to move.

The key is to stay calm, check the injury, and make smart choices from there.

You might be cut, scraped, bruised, or even dealing with a twisted ankle. Whatever the injury is, your job is to slow down, focus, and take things one step at a time.

Step 1: Stay Still and Breathe

The very first thing to do after you get hurt is to stop moving and take a moment to breathe. Even if you tripped, slipped, or bumped into something, give your body a chance to catch up with your brain.

Breathe slowly. In through your nose, out through your mouth. Remind yourself: "I'm okay. I can handle this."
This pause helps you think clearly instead of rushing into decisions or moving too quickly.

Ask yourself:

- Am I in a safe place?
- Can I move without causing more pain?
- What hurts the most?

Don't rush. Your body needs a minute to settle before your brain can make good decisions.

Step 2: Check the Injury
After calming down, gently look at the part of your body that hurts. It might be bleeding, swelling, or just sore.

Move slowly. Take your time. Use your hands and your eyes to figure out what's going on.

If you have a small cut or scrape, rinse it with clean water if you can, then press a cloth against it until the bleeding stops. If it's a sprained ankle or wrist, try not to move it too much. Wrap it with a piece of cloth or bandana for support.

If you bumped your head, sit down and rest. Stay awake, breathe slowly, and pay attention to how you feel. A headache or a little soreness is okay. But if you start to feel dizzy, confused, or very sleepy, don't move. You need to focus on getting help or being found.

If it's a:
Small cut or scrape: Wash with clean water (if possible), pat dry, and cover with a bandage or clean cloth

Bruise: Rest and don't put pressure on it. Ice would help, but if you don't have any, stay still and protect it

Sprained ankle or wrist: Don't walk on it right away. Wrap it with a bandana or shirt for support

Deeper cut: Apply pressure with cloth or gauze until bleeding slows

Bump to the head: Sit still. Stay awake and pay attention to how you feel

If you start feeling dizzy, sick to your stomach, or very sleepy, you might need serious help. That's your sign to rest and use a signal to get attention fast.

Step 3: Decide if You Should Stay or Move

If you're badly hurt, stay put.

Set up a shelter, make yourself comfortable, and start signaling. Use sound and visual signals as often as you can (whistle, flashlight, bright gear, or ground symbols).

If the injury is minor and you're not far from a safe place or water, move slowly and carefully. Use a walking stick, crawl if needed, or make a splint to support your body.

Don't push it.

If it hurts more when you move, stop. You don't want to turn a small injury into a big one.

Stay if:

- You feel dizzy, weak, or in too much pain
- The injury gets worse when you try to move
- You're unsure how far the nearest help is

Move slowly if:

- The injury is minor
- You feel steady on your feet
- You're close to shelter, water, or an open space

Step 4: Keep Yourself Comfortable
Once you've made your decision, do everything you can to stay safe and steady.

If you're staying in place, make a comfortable seat or bed from your backpack, jacket, or leaves. Protect yourself from cold, wind, or rain. If you have water, take small sips. Rest. Let your body relax and begin to heal.

You can also focus your mind by keeping busy. Rearrange your gear. Add extra sticks to your shelter. Practice your breathing or repeat a calming phrase. All of this helps you stay in control.

To stay comfortable:

- Sip water if you have it
- Use leaves or gear to stay warm
- Rest your injury and breathe calmly
- Focus on small tasks to pass time and stay positive

Being alone and hurt can feel like the scariest part of survival, but you're not helpless. You have your brain. You have your body. And you've learned skills to care for yourself until help arrives.

Pain will pass. Help will come. But how you handle those moments in between, that's what makes you strong.

What to Do If You See a Wild Animal

You're walking through the forest, the sun is filtering through the trees, and suddenly, you see it. A wild animal.

Your heart might skip a beat. You might freeze in place. You might even feel a little excited. That's okay! Wild animals are part of the adventure. But they also need to be treated with care and respect. Most animals **don't want to hurt you**, they just want to be left alone. If you act calm and smart, chances are, they'll walk away on their own.

This page will help you understand what to do when you see a wild animal and how to stay safe, confident, and in control.

Rule #1: Don't Run

This is the most important survival rule when it comes to wild animals: **never run**.

Running triggers an instinct in many animals to chase. Even if they weren't planning to bother you, seeing you run can make them think you're prey. So instead, take a deep breath and stand still.

When you don't move suddenly, the animal has a chance to look at you and realize: "This isn't a threat." You can take one slow step back if needed, but always keep your eyes on the animal without staring it down. Turning your back or sprinting away is how accidents happen.

If You See a Large Animal (Like a Bear or Moose)

If you spot a bear or another large creature in the wild, it's normal to feel a surge of nervous energy. But the best response is to freeze, breathe, and observe.

If the animal is far away, your best move is to stay quiet and still. **Let it pass.** Animals like bears and moose will usually mind their own business if you give them space.

If it's closer, here's what to do:

- Don't run or scream.
- Speak in a soft, low voice and slowly wave your arms above your head.
- Begin backing away slowly.
- Keep facing the animal, but avoid staring directly into its eyes.
- Never get between a mother and her babies. That's when even peaceful animals can become protective and aggressive.

If the animal starts moving toward you and looks aggressive, try to make yourself look **big and loud**. Raise your arms, shout in a deep voice, and stomp. Most animals will back off if they think you're not easy to mess with.

Important: Only play dead if you're facing a grizzly bear and it's charging. Otherwise, stay tall and stand your ground.

If You See a Snake

Snakes are quiet, quick, and often well-camouflaged. That means you might not notice one until it's right near your foot. Don't panic, most snakes are not looking to attack.

If you spot a snake:

- Stop exactly where you are.
- Slowly take one or two steps backward.
- Give the snake a way to escape. Don't try to touch or scare it off.

Watch the ground more carefully moving forward, especially near rocks or fallen logs.

Snakes bite only when they feel threatened. If you stay calm and give them space, they'll usually slither away on their own.

If You See a Wild Dog, Coyote, or Fox

These animals are often seen near campsites or wooded areas. They may be curious, but they don't usually want to get close.

If one is watching you:

- Stand tall. Don't crouch down or look small.
- Clap your hands, stomp your feet, and use a loud voice.
- Wave your arms slowly to look bigger.
- Back away without turning your back.

Don't leave food out at your shelter or campsite. That's what draws wild animals in. Tie up your snacks or keep them sealed in your backpack and away from where you sleep.

If You See a Small Animal

Squirrels, raccoons, rabbits, and birds might dart across your path or rustle in nearby bushes. These animals aren't dangerous, but you should still treat them with caution.

Don't try to feed them or pet them. Wild animals can carry diseases or become aggressive if they feel cornered.

And if a small animal acts strange, like walking in circles or coming too close, it could be sick. In that case, slowly move away and don't touch it.

What NOT to Do

There are some rules that apply to every wild animal you might meet:

Don't run. Running makes you look like prey.
Don't get close. Even a "friendly-looking" animal might bite or scratch.
Don't feed it. This can teach animals to see humans as food sources, which can be dangerous for everyone.
Don't try to take pictures up close. Stay safe first—take pictures from far away if it's safe to do so.

❌**Don’t run.**❌

Running makes you look like prey.

❌**Don’t get close.**❌

Don’t get close. Even a “friendly-looking” animal might bite or scratch.

❌**Don't feed it.**❌

This can teach animals to see humans as food sources, which can be dangerous for everyone.

❌**Don’t try to take pictures up close.**❌

Stay safe first. Take pictures from far away if it’s safe to do so.

The Wild Is Their Home

Remember, you're a visitor in nature.
These animals live here, and most of them just want to be left alone.

If you show respect, stay calm, and give them space, you can enjoy the experience of seeing wildlife, without putting yourself or the animal at risk.

And if you do feel afraid? That's okay. Take a breath, stand tall, and remember, you've trained for this. You know what to do.

What to Do If You Get Lost

You're walking along a trail. The trees rustle. The wind feels good. And then suddenly, you stop. You look around.

Something feels wrong.

You don't see your group.
You're not sure which way is forward or backward.
Your heart beats faster.
You might be lost.

It's okay. It happens.

Getting lost in the wild feels scary, but it doesn't have to be dangerous; not if you use your brain, your breath, and your training.

Let's walk through what to do, step by step.

Step 1: Freeze and Focus

The moment you realize you might be lost, stop.
Don't walk in circles. Don't rush forward. Don't call out right away. Just freeze and take a long, deep breath.

Your brain works best when it's calm. So before you do anything else, remind yourself:
"I'm okay. I'm not in danger. I know what to do."

Even experienced hikers and explorers have gotten lost. What makes them safe is what they did next.

Step 2: Use What You Already Know

You've already learned how to:

- Stay calm
- Observe your surroundings
- Make a signal
- Use the S.T.O.P. method
- Decide when to move and when to stay

This is the moment you put all of that together.
Look around slowly.

Do you recognize anything? Did you pass a stream, a big tree, a camp sign? Listen. Do you hear voices, a fire crackling, or a whistle?

If nothing feels familiar, and you're not sure which way to go, **don't guess.** Stay put.

If you remember a clear path just a short distance behind you, and you're 100% sure how to retrace your steps, you can move carefully. But if you're even a little unsure—it's safer to stop and be found.

Step 3: Pick a Safe Spot to Wait

If you're staying in place, make yourself a safe, visible, and comfortable place to wait. This doesn't have to be a full shelter, just a spot where you can sit or lie down, protected from wind or rain.

Look for:

- Flat, dry ground
- Shade or cover from trees or rocks
- Nearby sticks, leaves, or gear to sit on
- A spot where searchers can see you from a distance

Set out bright objects (like your jacket or backpack), wave if you see movement, and use your whistle or flashlight every few minutes.

Step 4: Stay Warm, Stay Visible, Stay Calm
While you wait, take care of yourself.

- Sip water if you have it
- Rest, even if you're nervous
- Keep your body warm and dry with extra layers or padding
- Don't waste energy pacing or worrying

If it's getting late, gather soft materials and prepare to stay put through the night. You've already learned how to build basic shelter. This is where those skills come in handy.

You're not helpless.
You're prepared.

Final Words of Encouragement
Being lost isn't a failure, it's a chance to use your training.
Your job isn't to "figure it all out."
Your job is to stay calm, stay safe, and stay visible so others can find you.

Remember:
You're not alone. Someone is looking for you.
And you're making it easier for them to get to you.

How to Find Your Way Back If You Really Have to Move

Most of the time, staying in one place is the safest thing you can do. But what if you're in real danger from cold, weather, or wild animals? What if your shelter spot isn't safe anymore, or you're certain you passed a trail just a short time ago?

In these rare cases, you may need to move. But moving without a plan is risky.

So if you must go, here's how to do it smartly, calmly, and safely.

Choose a Direction, But Only One
Before taking even one step, think carefully. Ask yourself what direction you were heading before, or whether you remember seeing any familiar objects like a big tree, a bend in a stream, or a rocky hill.

Only move if:

- You are sure which direction you came from
- You haven't gone far from the trail or group
- You believe you can safely get back to a known landmark

Once you decide on a direction, commit to it. Wandering back and forth or constantly changing direction leads people deeper into the unknown.

Leave Clues Behind You
As you move, create a trail that others can follow, and that you can use to get back if needed. This also helps rescuers find you faster.

You can leave signs like:

- Stacking rocks or sticks in patterns
- Tying fabric or string to branches
- Scratching arrows into dirt or bark
- Breaking small branches to mark your path

These markers don't need to be fancy, they just need to stand out.

Walk with Awareness

Don't rush. Every step should be careful and purposeful. You don't want to get injured while trying to escape being lost.

As you move, pay attention to:

- The ground: Watch for holes, sharp rocks, or uneven slopes
- What's behind you: Turn around every few minutes to track your trail
- Unusual shapes, smells, or sounds: They might be clues to people, water, or paths

Take breaks often. Use those moments to re-check your direction, sip water, and stay alert.

Be Ready to Stop Again

Moving doesn't mean you have to keep moving forever. If you no longer feel sure of your direction, or you get tired, or things begin to feel less safe, you can stop.

There's no rule that says once you start, you can't change your mind. Good survivors know how to pause, rethink, and adjust.

Final Reminder:
If you must move, move like a tracker: focused, observant, and patient.
This isn't about getting somewhere fast. It's about getting there wisely.

Even if you take just twenty steps in the right direction, that may be enough to get you back to safety, or closer to being found.

How to Make a Basic Survival Map

You don't need to be a cartographer (that's a fancy word for map-maker) to sketch a survival map. In fact, when you're out in the wild, a simple hand-drawn map can help you remember where you've been, plan where to go, and help rescuers understand what you've seen.

Your memory can blur when you're tired or stressed. Drawing things down—even on a leaf, stick, or dirt—helps turn confusion into clarity.

Why Maps Matter in Survival

When you're alone in nature, having a basic map:

- Helps you track your movements so you don't double back
- Shows where you've left signs or shelter
- Helps rescuers understand your trail if they find your notes or drawings
- Gives you a mental picture that brings calm and direction

Even if your map isn't perfect, it can help you feel more in control.

What You'll Need

You don't need fancy tools. Just use what you have:

- A notebook or scrap of paper
- A stick to draw in the dirt
- A piece of bark, a flat rock, or even your own palm
- A pencil, pen, charcoal, or anything that marks

If nothing else, draw with your finger in the soil.

What to Put on Your Map

Keep your map simple. It doesn't have to look like something from a classroom.
Just include the most important details:

- Where you are now (mark this clearly, it's your starting point)
- Any landmarks you've seen: big trees, rivers, rocks, clearings
- Paths you've taken or places you tried
- Shelter spots or places you've rested
- Signal areas where you've left signs or gear
- Direction of the sun if you know it (east/west)

Label these with symbols, arrows, or even made-up icons. As long as they make sense to you, they're useful.

Pro Tip: Combine Map + Memory

Before moving, glance at your map. If something you see doesn't match what you drew, pause. Maybe you veered off the trail, or maybe you forgot a landmark.

Use your map to:

- Choose a direction
- Stay calm
- Spot patterns
- Track how far you've gone

And when you stop to rest, update it. That way, if someone finds your map, it could help lead them right to you.

Think Like a Problem-Solver

Survival isn't just about building fires or finding water. It's about using your brain, especially when things go wrong. Getting cold? Can't find a trail? Out of snacks? The strongest tool you have isn't in your backpack.

It's in your head.

Problem-solving is what turns fear into action. It's how you stop being stuck and start being in control. Smart survivors don't always have all the answers, but they know how to ask the right questions.

What Makes a Good Problem-Solver?

It's not about being the fastest or the loudest. It's about being the most thoughtful when things get tricky.

Good problem-solvers:

- Stay calm under pressure
- Break big problems into small steps
- Think of more than one solution
- Try something, test it, and adjust if needed
- Don't let fear take over their thinking

Even if you've never been in a survival situation, you've solved problems before. Lost a toy? Got separated from your group at the mall? That moment of pause and "What should I do?"—that's where problem-solving begins.

Try This: Micro Problems

Let's warm up your brain with some quick "wild world" questions. There's no one perfect answer—just options you can think through.

1. You ran out of clean water.

What's your first move? Where could you look nearby? What tools do you have?

2. You dropped your flashlight and it broke.

What else can you use for light or to stay safe in the dark?

3. It's about to rain and you don't have a tent.

What can you use from nature or your gear to stay dry?

A 4-Step Survival Thinking Strategy

Whenever you're facing a problem—big or small—use this four-step tool.

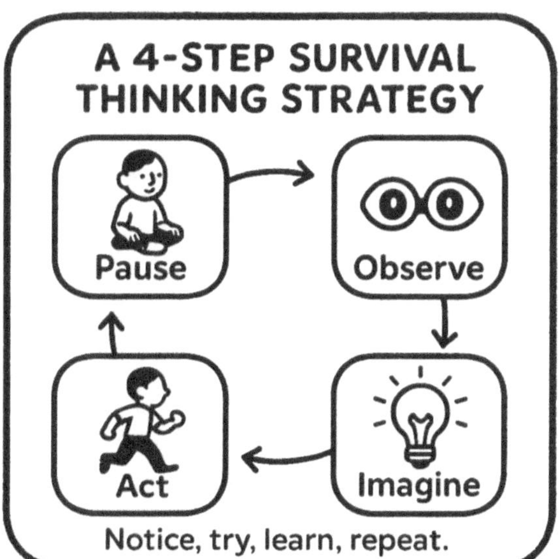

Every great problem-solver works in loops: notice, try, learn, repeat. It's not about being perfect. It's about being adaptable.

Challenge Mode: Create a Problem Chain

Draw a chain with 3–4 "what if" problems a survivor might face. Example:

"Rain starts" → "Wood is wet" → "Can't start fire" → "Feeling cold"

Now solve it! For each part of the chain, write down 1–2 possible solutions.

You just practiced systems thinking, just like real wilderness guides do.

Making Smart Decisions When You're Scared

You're alone in the woods. You hear a strange sound. You've lost sight of the path, and it's getting darker. Your heart starts pounding. Your chest tightens. You feel frozen.
This is fear, and **it's normal.**

The trick is not to get rid of fear. The trick is to know what to do with it.

Fear makes your brain jump to worst-case scenarios. It says things like:

"You can't do this." "You're in danger." "Run!"

But smart survivors know something important:
Your brain can feel fear and still make good decisions.

First, Understand What Fear Is Doing
When you're scared, your body flips into survival mode. Your heart beats faster. Your muscles tighten. Your thoughts race.
This is called the fight–flight–freeze response. It's your body getting ready for action—but it can also cloud your thinking.
When fear takes over, it can lead to:

- Rushing without planning
- Forgetting things you already know
- Making choices just to feel busy, not to stay safe
- Ignoring warning signs because your brain is in panic mode
-

You can't always control fear, but you can learn to slow it down.

Second, Reset Your Thinking

When fear floods in, hit pause. The best way to take back control is by using your breath.

Try this:

- Inhale slowly for four seconds
- Hold for two seconds
- Exhale slowly for six seconds
- Do it three times

This signals your brain:

"I'm not in danger. I'm still in charge."

Now your brain can shift from fear to focus.

Third, Ask Yourself Better Questions

Once you've slowed your breath, it's time to slow your thoughts. Ask yourself:

- What do I know for sure right now?
- What tools or skills do I have?
- What's one small action I can take next?
- What is my goal, and what step brings me closer?

Asking questions gives your brain a job. That helps turn fear into movement.

Fourth, Use Your Survival Tools

You've already learned how to:

- Make a plan
- Find shelter
- Signal for help
- Stay warm
- Think through a problem

Now's the time to use those tools, not let fear talk you out of them.

Fear says: “You’ll mess this up.”
You say: “I’ve practiced this. I know what to do.”

Final Thought

Being scared doesn’t make you weak.
It makes you human.

The strongest survivors aren’t the ones who feel nothing, they’re the ones who feel fear and choose wisely anyway.

You are not your fear.

You are your choices.

“What Would You Do? Challenge Pages

Now that you’ve learned how to stay calm, solve problems, and make smart decisions; even when things feel scary—it’s time to put those skills into practice.

These challenge pages aren’t tests. There are no right or wrong answers.

They’re here to help you slow down, think clearly, and trust your survival brain.

Imagine each scene. Picture it in your mind.
Then answer honestly: **What would you do? Why?**

You can write, draw, or just think it through.

Challenge #1: Lost in the Forest

You've been walking with your group through a trail. At one point, you stop to tie your shoe. When you stand up, the group is gone. No voices. No path.
You're surrounded by trees and tall grass.

What would you do in the first five minutes?

- Would you move or stay put?
- Would you shout or stay quiet?
- What tools do you have?
- What's your goal?

Challenge #2: No Water Left

It's been a few hours since you drank anything. Your bottle is empty. The sun is out. You're starting to feel tired and thirsty. There's no stream nearby.

What could you try to do?

- Where might you look for water?
- How would you stay calm and conserve energy?
- What tools could help you collect or purify water?

Challenge #3: Storm Rolling In

The clouds turn dark. The wind picks up. You hear thunder in the distance. You don't have a tent, and you're still a short walk away from your camp.

How would you prepare before the rain hits?

- Where would you go for shelter?
- What could you use to stay dry?
- What would you do with your gear?

Challenge #4: Night Comes Early

You've been walking most of the day and didn't realize how late it's gotten. The sun is setting fast. You don't have a flashlight. You're not sure if you're still on the path.

How would you stay safe in the dark?

- Would you keep walking or stop?
- How could you stay warm?
- What would you do to be found?

How to Read Clouds and Know What's Coming

The sky isn't just a ceiling over your head; it's a warning system.
When you're in the wild, the clouds, wind, and light around you can help you guess what's on the way... even before you feel the first raindrop.

Learning how to read the sky doesn't require fancy tools. Just your eyes, your memory, and a little bit of practice.

What Clouds Can Tell You
Clouds form when water in the air gathers together. But different clouds form in different ways, and they often give you clues about what kind of weather is coming.

Let's look at the main types you might see:

Big and fluffy (cumulus)
These clouds look like cotton candy. When they're bright white and high in the sky, they usually mean good weather.

Tall and dark (cumulonimbus)
These are storm clouds. They grow upward like towers. If you see one with a flat top like an anvil, a storm is likely on the way.

Thin and wispy (cirrus)
These clouds float high and look like streaks or feathers. They often come before a change in weather, like rain within the next day.

Flat and gray (stratus)
These clouds can cover the whole sky and make everything feel dull. They bring light rain or drizzle that might last a while.

What to Watch For
Survivors pay attention to the sky not just once—but over time.

Look up often and ask:

- Are clouds getting taller or darker?
- Is the wind picking up or changing direction?
- Did the air suddenly feel colder or more damp?

Even if you're not a weather expert, these changes mean it's time to find shelter or adjust your plan.

Staying Safe in Lightning, Wind, and Storms

The wild is full of surprises, and the weather can change fast. What was a sunny afternoon can turn into thunder, wind, or pouring rain before you even realize it. That's why good survivors don't just watch the clouds. They know how to respond when storms arrive.

Whether it's lightning flashing across the sky, trees bending in high winds, or a heavy downpour making everything slippery, the most important thing to remember is this:
You can't control the weather, but you can control your response.

Lightning: Bright, Loud, and Dangerous

Lightning is beautiful, but it's also extremely powerful. It doesn't have to strike close to be dangerous. If you can hear thunder, lightning is close enough to hurt you.

If you hear thunder or see lightning:

- **Leave open areas immediately.** Don't stay in fields, lakes, or hilltops.
- **Stay away from tall objects.** Trees, towers, and poles can attract lightning.
- **Avoid metal.** That includes fences, tent poles, and tools.
- **Crouch low if you're caught in the open.** Don't lie down, just squat with your heels together and your head down.

Shelter is best. If you can get under a low rock shelf, inside a thick forest (not under the tallest tree), or into a low, dry spot, do it quickly and stay there until the thunder passes.

Wind: Invisible but Powerful

Strong wind might not look scary, but it can break branches, knock over tents, and blow debris into your path.

In high winds:

- Stay out of open clearings where things can fly at you
- Don't camp under trees with dead branches. Wind can snap them
- Tie down your gear and protect your fire (or put it out completely)
- Use natural barriers like rocks or hillsides to block the wind

Even if wind doesn't bring rain, it can chill your body fast, especially if you're damp or sweating. Stay warm, layer up, and keep your shelter tight.

Heavy Rain: Wet, Cold, and Sneaky

Rain doesn't seem dangerous at first, but too much of it can lead to hypothermia, slick terrain, and poor visibility. If you're not prepared, rain makes everything harder.

If heavy rain starts:

- Don't stay in low areas, they can flood quickly
- Use a poncho, tarp, or trash bag as a rain shield
- Build shelter that angles water away from where you sit or sleep
- Keep your firewood and matches dry by storing them high and wrapped
- Avoid rivers, streams, or dry creek beds, as they can swell fast

Rain is also noisy, which means rescuers might not hear your calls or whistles. Make sure your visual signals are still visible if you're stuck waiting out a storm.

Weather Watching for Survival (With Sky Charts!)

Every good survivalist has a superpower, and it's not what you might think. It's not building fires or catching fish. It's this: watching the sky and noticing small changes before they become big problems.

Weather isn't random. The clouds, wind, temperature, and even smells in the air are always telling a story. You just have to learn how to listen.

How to Be a Sky Watcher

Most people only look at the sky when it starts to rain. But survival thinkers look long before that.

Here's how to start training your observation muscles:

- Each day, ask yourself:
- What type of clouds do I see?
- How fast are they moving?
- What direction is the wind blowing?
- Does the air feel warm or cold on my skin?
- Are birds flying low or high?
- Can I smell rain or feel extra dampness in the air?

These tiny clues can help you predict what's coming, and take action before the weather changes.

Sky Log Activity

Create your own Weather Watch Log with just a notebook or a printable chart. Each day, record:

- Date & time
- Cloud type (draw it or describe it!)
- Wind (strong, gentle, none)

- Sky color (blue, hazy, grey, glowing)
- Prediction: What do you think the weather will be in 3 hours?

Then come back and write what really happened.
Did you get it right?
That's how survival skills become second nature; through practice.

Sky Chart Basics

Make your own mini chart to help remember common cloud meanings:

Cloud Type	What It Looks Like	What It Might Mean
Cumulus	Fluffy, bright white	Fair weather, for now
Cirrus	Wispy, high in the sky	Change coming within a day
Stratus	Flat and gray	Drizzle, light rain
Cumulonimbus	Tall, dark, tower-like	Thunderstorm or heavy rain soon

You can draw these in your notebook or print a card to carry in your kit. The sky becomes a little less mysterious when you've got this cheat sheet in your pocket.

MY WEATHER WATCH LOG

DATE & TIME: ______________________

CLOUD TYPE:

WIND: ☐ none ☐ gentle ☐ strong

SKY COLOR ☐ blue ☐ gray
☐ hazy

PREDICTION (What will the weather be in 3 hours?)

ACTUAL WEATHER
(What really happened?)

____

____

____

How to Follow Animal Trails and Human Tracks

Sometimes, in the wild, the path isn't marked with signs or arrows. But the land still tells a story, you just have to know how to read it.

When animals or people move through the woods, they leave behind small clues: bent grass, broken twigs, disturbed soil, a smudge on a rock. These little details are called tracks and signs, and learning to spot them can help you:

- Follow an animal trail
- Backtrack to your own campsite
- Stay alert for nearby people
- Avoid danger by knowing what passed through before you
-

Tracking isn't just a skill. It's a way of paying attention.

How to Spot a Trail in the Wild

Animals often take the same routes again and again, wearing narrow paths through grass or brush. These are called game trails.

To recognize them, look for:

- Flattened grass in straight or curved lines
- Fur or feathers caught on bark or branches
- Twigs snapped at the same height
- Repeated hoof or paw prints in mud or soft dirt
- Scat (animal droppings) along a path

A clear animal trail may lead to water, food sources, or safe sleeping areas. But remember, if animals are using it, predators might be too, so always observe first before following closely.

Tracking Human Footsteps
Sometimes, you might be looking for someone from your group, or trying to retrace your own steps. Human footprints are different from animal tracks: usually larger, flatter, and more uniform.

To follow a human trail, look for:

- Shoe treads in soft dirt or sand
- Crushed leaves or displaced rocks that show weight was applied
- Broken spiderwebs at chest level (a sign someone passed recently)
- Unnatural items like string, trash, or tool marks
- Parallel signs like scuff marks from dragging a backpack or stick

If you're leaving a trail on purpose for someone to follow you, walk with intention. Leave clear footprints, stack small rocks, or tie fabric to low branches.

Try This: Backyard Tracker
Pick a small area in a yard, park, or trail. Spend 5–10 minutes looking carefully at the ground.
Ask yourself:

- Can I see which direction someone (or something) moved?
- What kind of weight or stride do the prints suggest?
- Did anything look out of place or recently moved?
-

You don't need to be a wildlife expert. You just need to notice.

The forest doesn't speak in words, but it always leaves signs.

How to Leave a Trail That Leads Rescuers to You
If you ever get lost or have to move through the wild, you don't want to disappear. You want to be findable.

That means thinking ahead, not just about where you're going, but how someone could follow behind and reach you.

Leaving a trail doesn't mean tossing trash or shouting every five minutes. It means creating a quiet message that says:
"I was here. I went this way. Come find me."

Trail Signs That Help People Track You
Survivors leave signs that are clear, consistent, and easy to spot. If someone's looking for you, they'll know what to watch for.

Smart trail signs include:

- Broken branches at chest height (snapped cleanly to mark direction)

Rocks stacked in a triangle or line on the trail

- Sticks shaped into arrows pointing the way you're going
- Pieces of cloth or string tied to trees
- Symbols on the ground, like an "X" or "I'm okay" sign made from sticks or stones

Each sign should repeat every few steps. Don't rely on just one.

Use What You Have
You don't need special gear to make a trail.
You can use:

- Bandanas, shoelaces, or ripped fabric
- Charcoal or dirt to mark rocks
- Natural objects like leaves, pinecones, or sticks

Just be careful not to strip too much from the environment. The goal is to stand out, not destroy what's around you.

🚫 **What Not to Do**
Not all marks are helpful. Some things might confuse rescuers or get washed away easily.

Avoid:

- Drawing tiny marks in the mud that could vanish in rain
- Moving so fast your signs are spread too far apart
- Changing directions without explaining it (e.g., no arrow turn)
- Covering old signs with new ones (it gets messy fast)

Every sign should build a path, not scatter a puzzle.

Leave a Note if You Can
If you have paper, a notepad, or even a food wrapper, you can write a quick message and leave it in a dry spot (like under a rock or in a clear bag).

Write your name, the date, where you're heading, and how you feel (okay, injured, etc.)

That one note could save hours of searching.

Try This: Make a Practice Trail

In your backyard or a park, create a short rescue trail:

- Leave an arrow with sticks
- Tie a cloth to a branch
- Stack three stones in a pattern
- Add a message card at the end

Now have a friend or sibling follow it. Were your signs easy to see?
If not, how could you make them better?

You're not just surviving. You're helping someone find you. And that might be the most important thing you ever do.

Useful Knots (with Diagrams)

Knots aren't just for sailors and rock climbers. In the wild, knowing how to tie the right knot can help you build a shelter, hang food safely, fix broken gear, or even make a rescue signal.

The best knots are simple, strong, and easy to untie, even after they've been pulled tight.

Here are four survival knots every adventurer should know, plus what each one is good for.

1. Square Knot (a.k.a. Reef Knot)

What it's for:

- Tying two ropes together
- Bundling wood or gear
- Making bandages or slings

How to tie it:

Left over right and pull tight, then right over left and pull tight.

How to test it:

The knot should lie flat and hold strong when both ends are pulled. If it slips or twists into a different shape, try again more slowly.

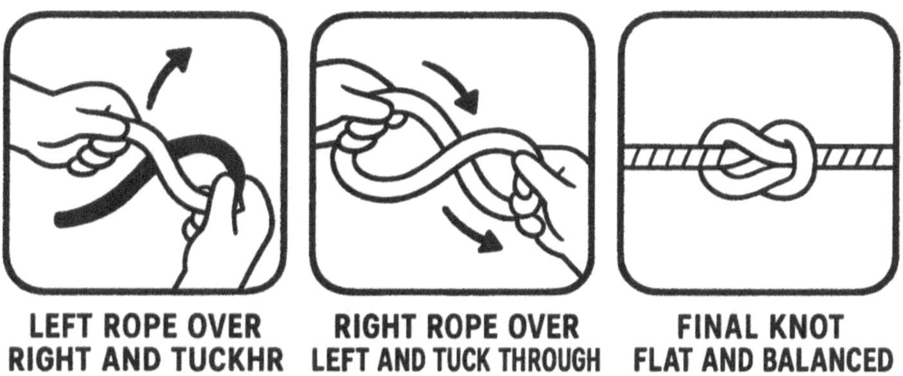

2. Bowline Knot (The Rescue Loop)

What it's for:

- Making a secure loop that doesn't tighten
- Pulling or lifting people or gear
- Attaching rope to a post or tree

How to tie it:

Make a small loop. Bring the loose end up through the loop, around the back of the rope, and back down through the loop.

How to remember:

"The rabbit comes out of the hole, around the tree, and back down the hole."

3. Clove Hitch (Fast + Adjustable)

<u>What it's for:</u>

- Tying rope to a pole, stick, or tree
- Holding up shelter walls or tarps
- Temporary gear hanging

<u>How to tie it:</u>

Wrap the rope around a post. Cross over and wrap again above the first loop. Tuck the end under the second wrap and pull tight.

<u>Why it's great:</u>

It's quick to tie and adjust, but it might slip under very heavy loads, so always double-check.

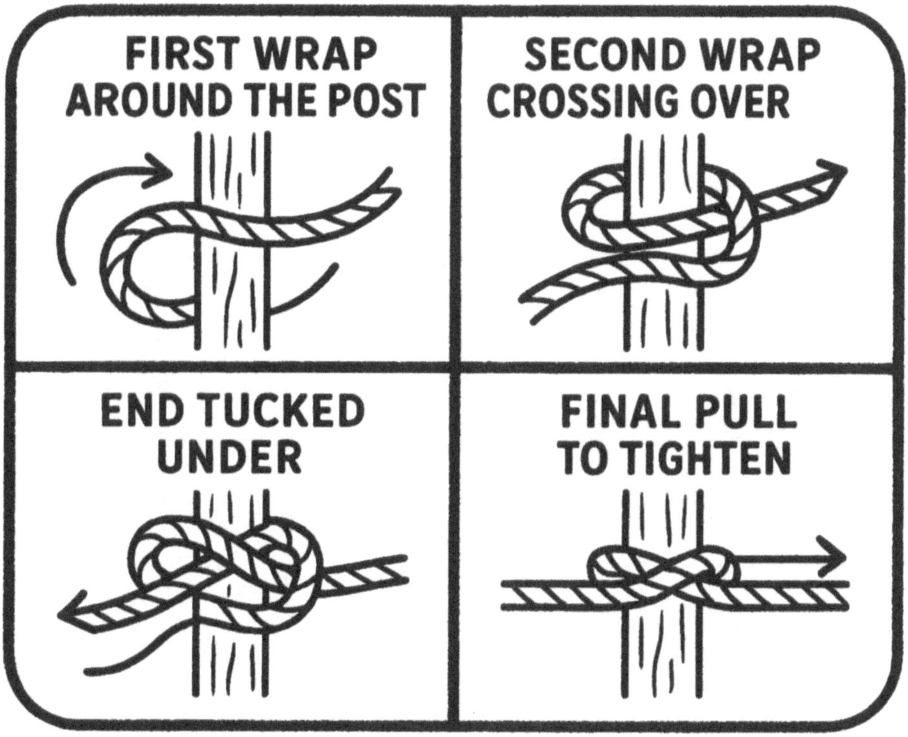

4. Figure Eight Knot (The Stopper)

What it's for:

- Making a strong stopper at the end of a rope
- Preventing fraying
- Holding loops together when weight is added

How to tie it:

Make a loop. Wrap the loose end behind the standing rope and back through the loop, just like drawing the number 8.

Bonus tip:

This knot is super strong and easy to untie—even after being pulled tight.

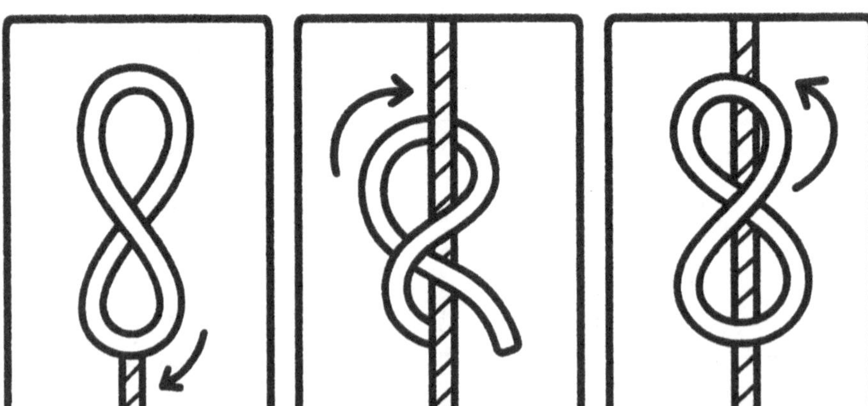

Making a loop | **Wrapping the end around the standing rope** | **Bringing it back through the loop to form a clean "8'**

Food: What's Safe to Eat and What's Not

When you're hungry in the wild, it's tempting to eat the first thing you find: berries, mushrooms, leaves, or even bugs. But not everything that looks like food is safe.

In fact, eating the wrong thing is more dangerous than eating nothing at all. Your body can go several days without food, but just one bite of the wrong plant or spoiled meat could make you sick or weak.

That's why survival thinkers follow one key rule:
"If you're not 100% sure it's safe—don't eat it."

Things That Might Be Safe (But Only If You're Sure)
With proper training and adult guidance, some of these may be safe to eat:

- Wild berries (blackberries, mulberries, or blueberries)

Edible leaves like dandelion greens

- Nuts like acorns (if boiled first to remove bitterness)
- Roots or tubers like cattail (edible in small parts, when prepared properly)

But even these can look similar to poisonous plants. Don't rely on guessing. Learn with a guidebook or adult before ever trying them.

🚫 Dangerous Foods to Always Avoid
These are never safe unless you are trained, and should be avoided in all kid-level survival situations:

- Mushrooms – even experts make mistakes
- Berries you don't recognize – red and white ones are often toxic

- Bright or shiny leaves – often signal poison
- Milky sap or bitter-tasting plants
- Raw meat or fish – can carry bacteria or parasites
- Spoiled or stinky food – a sign it's rotten and unsafe

Also avoid plants near roads, farms, or polluted water, as they may carry chemicals or waste.

Final **Reminder**

Food helps you survive. But in the wild, knowledge is the real nourishment.
If you're not sure, wait. Rest. Drink water.
It's better to be a hungry survivor than a sick one.

Your Survival Badge & Certificate of Completion

You've done more than just read a book.
You've learned how to think clearly in scary situations.
You've practiced real survival skills—like making shelter, finding safe water, solving problems, and working with nature instead of against it.

Most people never prepare for tough situations.
But you have.

You've taken the first step toward becoming someone who can stay calm, take care of themselves, and even help others when things go wrong.

Whether you're in your backyard, on a hike, or just solving everyday problems, these skills will stay with you.

What You've Learned:

- Survival thinking and calm decision-making
- How to stay safe when lost or alone
- Building and using tools from nature
- Tracking signs, reading the sky, and staying warm
- Signaling for help, storing water, and protecting yourself
- And most of all: trusting your own instincts and brain

SURVIVAL SKILLS FOR KIDS

CERTIFICATE OF COMPLETION

AWARDED TO

____

For completing all core survival lessons with courage and curiosity.

____

DATE

JUNIOR SURVIVOR